FEARSOME, SCARY, AND CREEPY ANIMALS

Scary Sharks

Elaine Landau

Enslow Publishers, Inc.

40 Industrial Road   PO Box 38
Box 398   Aldershot
Berkeley Heights, NJ 07922 Hants GU12 6BP
USA   UK

http://www.enslow.com

For Jerry, Bianca, and Abraham

Library of Congress Cataloging-in-Publication Data

Landau, Elaine.
 Scary sharks / Elaine Landau.
  p. cm. — (Fearsome, scary, and creepy animals)
 Summary: Introduces sharks and why they sometimes attack humans, and
tells of some real-life shark attacks.
 Includes bibliographical references (p.   ).
 ISBN 0-7660-2058-4 (hardcover : alk. paper)
 1. Sharks—Juvenile literature. 2. Shark attacks—Juvenile
literature. [1. Sharks. 2. Shark attacks.] I. Title. II. Series.
 QL638.9 .L35 2003
 597.3—dc21
                                        2002006938

Printed in the United States of America

10 9 8 7 6 5 4 3 2

To Our Readers: We have done our best to make sure all Internet addresses in this book were active and appropriate when we went to press. However, the author and the publisher have no control over and assume no liability for the material available on those Internet sites or on other Web sites they may link to. Any comments or suggestions can be sent by e-mail to comments@enslow.com or to the address on the back cover.

Illustration Credits: © 1999 Artville, LLC, pp. 34 (bottom), 35; © Corel Corporation, pp. 11, 33, 36, 37; Arbogast Family, p. 7; Digital Vision, pp. 5, 12, 13, 14, 16, 17, 19, 21, 22 (top), 24, 28, 29, 31, 34 (top), 41; Hemera Technologies, Inc., pp. ii, iii, 18, 27, 30; John Bavaro, p. 4; Mark Foley/Associated Press, p. 6; Matt May/Associated Press, p. 15; National Aeronautics and Space Administration, p. 9; Picture Quest, pp. i, 10, 25; Richard Silverberg, p. 20; Seapics.com, p. 22 (bottom), 23, 26. Borders © Corel Corporation.

Cover Illustration: Picture Quest

Contents

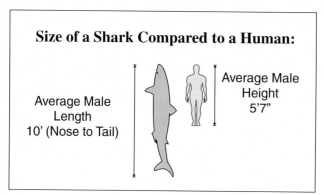

Size of a Shark Compared to a Human:

Average Male
Length
10' (Nose to Tail)

Average Male
Height
5'7"

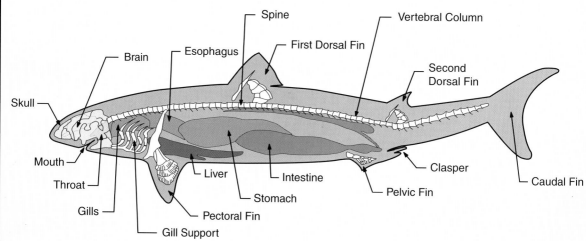

Spine

Vertebral Column

Esophagus

First Dorsal Fin

Brain

Second
Dorsal Fin

Skull

Mouth

Liver

Clasper

Throat

Intestine

Caudal Fin

Gills

Stomach

Pelvic Fin

Pectoral Fin

Gill Support

Most sharks have a rounded, torpedo-shaped body.
This shape helps them to swim quickly through
the water.

1. A Day at the Beach

It was a beautiful July day. Eight-year-old Jessie Arbogast was at a Florida beach. His brothers, sister, some cousins, and uncle were there, too. Everyone had enjoyed the sun and surf.

It was just after sunset, but no one was ready to go home. The children were still swimming. Jessie, his brothers, and cousins were in shallow water. They were about fifteen feet from the shore.

Something in the water brushed past Jessie's brother. The boys were not sure what it was. But they were about to find out. Seconds later, it happened. A 200-pound, seven-foot-long bull shark attacked Jessie. "He's got me!"

A bull shark, like this one, attacked Jessie Arbogast.

Jessie cried out from the water. "Get him off! Get him off me!"

Jessie's uncle, Vance Flosenzier, was on the beach. He heard the boy's screams and saw blood in the water. Flosenzier, along with another man, ran to help the boy. They took him out of the water. The men also grabbed the shark. They wrestled it to the shore.

Pensacola Beach, Florida, was the site of the shark attack on Jessie Arbogast.

The shark had bitten off Jessie's arm. It ripped into part of his right leg, too. The boy had lost a lot of blood.

Help came quickly. A medical emergency helicopter landed at the spot. It would take Jessie to the hospital. But the rescue team did not leave right away. The medics had an important question—where was Jessie's arm? There was a chance that doctors at the hospital might be able to reattach it.

Jessie's arm was in the shark's mouth. The large bull shark had been left on the shore, and it was still thrashing on the beach.

Jessie Arbogast was only eight years old at the time of the attack.

National Park Service Ranger Jared Klein had arrived on the scene. He knew what he had to do. He shot the shark in the head. Then, he pulled open its jaws. Tony Thomas, an emergency medical technician at the beach, helped the ranger. He reached into the shark's mouth and pulled out the boy's arm. Thomas wrapped the limb in a towel. He packed it in ice. A police car came to the beach. The officer took Jessie's arm to the hospital.

A medical team was waiting for Jessie at the hospital. The boy was given blood. The doctors also looked at the torn arm. It was still in fairly good shape. They would try to reattach it.

Doctors worked through the night on Jessie. It paid off. The operation was a success.

Word of the shark attack spread. It became a national news story. Florida Governor Jeb Bush visited Jessie in the hospital to wish him well. The whole country hoped Jessie would recover. He pulled through, but has still not fully recovered.

Did You Know...

There are about 370 different species of shark.

Everyone has heard about horrible shark attacks. Yet, they are not very common. Most shark attacks on humans are accidents. Sharks do not view people as dinner. But sometimes, sharks mistake people for their prey (what they usually eat).

Lately, shark attacks have increased throughout the world. There were thirty-seven reported shark attacks in 1990. By 2001, the number rose to fifty-five.

Jeb Bush, governor of Florida, went to visit Jessie Arbogast in the hospital.

The numbers continue to rise. There is a reason for this. There are not more sharks in the water, but there are more swimmers, divers, and boaters. That means more chances for mistakes.

Nevertheless, the attack on Jessie Arbogast was unusual. Robert Hueter summed it up. Hueter is the director of the Center for Shark Research at Mote Marine Laboratory in Sarasota, Florida. He said, "The case of that little boy…was an out and out attack. These are rare. But they do happen ten to twelve times a year in the world. A large, aggressive shark will occasionally feed on us. It's because we're not. . . completely distasteful [bad tasting]."

The number of shark attacks has increased as more people go swimming, diving, and boating in the ocean.

2. All About Sharks

Sharks are meat-eating fish. They are not new to our waters—they have been around for more than 400 million years. They were here before dinosaurs.

Scientists are not sure how many species, or kinds, of sharks there are. They think that there are about 370 different types. All sharks are not alike. Some are quite large. A whale shark can be sixty feet long and weigh over fifty tons. That equals the weight of two full-grown African elephants! Yet, there are also six-inch-long sharks. These weigh a little over an ounce.

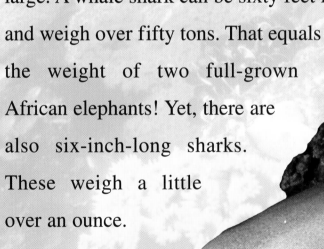

Nurse sharks often hide in the reef.

Sharks have different shapes, too. Most have rounded bodies that narrow at both ends. They look like torpedoes traveling through the water.

Sharks are interesting in other ways, as well.

Anatomy of a Shark

Skeleton

Most fish have bones. But sharks do not. Their skeletons are made up of a strong, rubbery material. It is called

Most sharks are torpedo-shaped.

cartilage. The shark's cartilage skeleton helps it to swim and turn easily. Humans have cartilage, too. Our noses and ears are made of cartilage.

Sharks can turn easily in the water because their skeletons are made up of cartilage instead of bones.

Tails and Fins

Some sharks are very fast swimmers. They can go as fast as forty miles an hour. The fastest, most powerful

swimmers have large, crescent-shaped tails. The top of this tail is longer than the bottom. This tail is also known as the caudal fin.

Sharks have a pair of stiff side fins, as well. These are called pectoral fins. They help to lift the shark in the water. Pectoral fins have been compared to airplane wings.

The dorsal fin is on the shark's back. It is a large, triangle-shaped fin. The dorsal fin is often seen above the surface of the water as the shark swims.

Swimmers can sometimes see the fin on the top of the shark's body sticking up out of the water.

Sometimes, swimmers see it. Then they know it is time to get out of the water! Some types of sharks have two dorsal fins. Sharks have two other types of fins, as well.

These are their pelvic and anal fins. Both types of fins help the shark move through the water.

Teeth and Scales

Many sharks have rows of teeth. But shark teeth are not like human teeth. They do not have roots to keep them firmly in the sharks' jaws. Sharks often break or lose teeth when biting. When a shark loses teeth from the front row, new ones move up from the row behind. These replace the missing ones. The teeth in the rows behind those move ahead, too. A shark's teeth are continually replaced. A single shark may lose as many as 30,000 teeth during its life.

Some sharks have pointed teeth. This tooth was removed from the hand of a swimmer after a shark attack.

Sharks rip chunks of meat off their prey. Then, they swallow the chunks whole.

Shark teeth come in different shapes. Some sharks have pointed teeth. Others have teeth with jagged edges. Sharks do not use their teeth to chew food. Their front row teeth rip off and crush chunks of their prey. Then they swallow their meal whole. Some shark jaws measure three feet across. They are lined with hundreds of knifelike teeth.

Sharks also have sharp, toothlike scales covering their skin. These are called denticles. A shark's skin is sharp enough to cut you. Like its teeth, its denticles are always being replaced.

Gills

Like people, fish need oxygen to live. Humans get oxygen from the air they breathe. Fish, including sharks, get oxygen from the water. They do this through organs called gills. Water enters the shark's mouth as it

Sharks do not need to come up out of the water for air. They get oxygen from the water.

swims. The water is forced over the shark's gills. The oxygen is removed through a system of blood vessels in the gills. These vessels are called capillaries. The water passes out through slits on both sides of the shark's head. Different types of sharks have from five to seven of these slits.

Senses

A shark's senses are extremely important. Its eyes help it spot prey. Sharks have a sharp sense of smell. They can smell a drop of blood in the water a quarter of a mile away. Sharks also have good hearing. This is especially true for low-pitched sounds. They can hear a fish struggling from a great distance.

Sharks have other ways to sense things, too. These include lateral line organs. Lateral line organs are rows of pores or holes along the sides of the shark's body. They contain cells that

detect (sense) movement. This helps the shark find its prey. Sharks are also able **Sharks can hear fish struggling from far away.** to detect electricity. Their heads contain pores or holes that lead to a complex system of tubes. The tubes are known as ampullae of Lorenzini. They are sensitive to electrical fields. This is helpful in hunting, as well. Every living animal gives off small amounts of

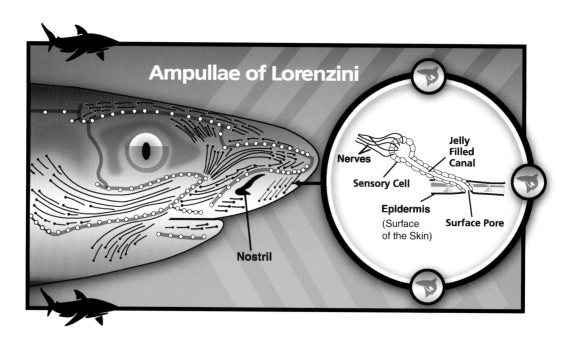

Ampullae of Lorenzini

Nerves

Jelly Filled Canal

Sensory Cell

Epidermis
(Surface of the Skin)

Surface Pore

Nostril

electricity. With the ampullae of Lorenzini, sharks can sense the electricity given off by their prey.

Staying Afloat

Most sharks must swim continuously. If they stop, they sink. This is not true for most other fish, which have gas-filled organs known as swim bladders. Swim bladders help keep fish afloat. Instead of swim bladders, sharks have large livers. Their livers are filled with oil.

Oil is lighter than water. This keeps sharks from sinking. Some shark livers can be up to 25 percent of their body weight. But this still is not enough to keep them afloat if they stop swimming.

What Sharks Attack Humans?

Nearly any large shark could attack a swimmer or diver. Yet, records show that only ten to twenty types have done so. Three sharks are most often involved in these attacks. These are the great white shark, the bull shark, and the tiger shark. Here is a closer look at each.

Sharks must swim constantly, or they will sink.

The great white is the largest fish predator in the world.

Great White Sharks

The great white shark is the world's largest fish predator. A predator is an animal that hunts other animals for food. Females sometimes grow to be nineteen-and-a-half feet long. Males may grow to fourteen-and-a-half feet.

A great white shark has about 3,000 teeth. These have jagged edges and are razor sharp. They are often compared to steak knives. A great white shark is not all white—only its underside is. Its top is gray. This helps it to blend with the sea.

Tiger Sharks

Tiger sharks are gray-brown on top. Young ones have dark stripes on their backs. That is why they are called

Tiger shark.

tiger sharks. The underside of a tiger shark is off-white. Tiger sharks are usually about ten feet long. However, some have grown twice that large. These sharks have jagged edged teeth. They are curved and quite sharp.

Bull Sharks

Bull sharks are gray on top and white underneath. These sharks are very aggressive. That means they are fierce and quick to attack. Female bull sharks are about ten feet long. Males are usually seven feet long.

The bull shark's lower teeth are like spikes. The lower teeth stab and hold its prey. Its upper teeth are shaped like triangles. These have jagged edges. They rip out the flesh.

Bull shark.

3. Shark Attack

It was a crisp autumn day. A great white shark was on the prowl. It would not have to wait long for its prey. An elephant seal was nearby. The shark moved in for the kill. Its victim never saw it coming. The great white dived down about thirty feet beneath the seal. The shark closed its jaws around the animal. The seal could not escape. After one large bite, it was dead.

This type of strike is called a sneak attack. The shark strikes without warning. A sneak attack can be deadly. It is one of three major kinds of shark attacks.

A second kind of strike is the bump-and-bite attack. Here the

Although such attacks are rare, sharks sometimes attack divers.

24

victim sees the shark coming. Usually, the shark circles the prey. It even bumps into it before biting. Both sneak attacks and bump-and-bite attacks are quite serious. Great whites, tiger sharks, and bull sharks cause most of these attacks.

In a sneak attack, a shark will strike without warning.

The third type of strike is the hit-and-run attack. Here, a small shark spots a swimmer's hand or foot in the water. It mistakes it for a fish. The shark takes a bite. It sees that this is not its usual prey, so the shark swims away. The attack victim is bitten but survives. Usually, only some stitches are needed. Several different types of sharks may be involved in these attacks. These include the black nose shark and the spinner shark.

Hit-and-run attacks are the most common type of shark attack. Michael Heidenreich knows what this is like—it happened to him. He was on vacation in South Carolina at the time. One evening, he decided to take a swim. He felt something tug at this leg in the water. It was a shark.

"There really wasn't much to it," Heidenreich said. "It just kind of took a chomp and left. There wasn't a lot of pain." Heidenreich had the wound treated. He had to use crutches for a few weeks, but his leg healed. That is how many hit-and-run shark attacks happen.

Black nose shark.

4. A Near Miss

Not everyone survives a shark attack. Some victims die. Others are badly hurt. That is what happened to Jolie Hamaliainen. She was swimming in the Caribbean Sea. Suddenly, she felt something slam up against her. It was a shark. Seconds later, she saw its head next to her shoulder. Her arm was already in its mouth. "I started to scream," she remembered. But the shark did not let go. It dragged her beneath the water.

Hamaliainen's husband was swimming with her. He tried to help. He grabbed the shark's fins with both hands. He kicked it, as well. Finally, Jolie escaped. She was badly hurt. She needed several operations to fully recover, but she lived.

One well-known shark attack victim is Rodney Fox. Fox was bitten while he was spear fishing off the coast of Australia. In spear fishing, the diver goes underwater and stabs fish with the blade of a spear gun.

The day Fox was attacked was special.

Even when divers go underwater in cages, sharks will sometimes still attack. The sharks may mistake the divers for their prey.

He was in a spear fishing contest. There were a lot of divers in the water. Many fish had been speared. That meant that there was also a lot of blood. Sharks are drawn to the smell of blood.

People sometimes use freshly killed fish as bait for shark-fishing, because sharks are drawn to the smell of blood.

A great white shark attacked Fox. There was no

warning. It seemed to crash into him. Its thrust sent Fox through the water and knocked his spear gun out of his hand. He would have to face the fearsome predator unarmed.

Great white shark.

The great white bit into Fox's shoulder and back. Fox struggled to get away. He punched the shark as hard as he could. But the great white would not let go. It shook Fox back and forth. It was as if the diver were a rag doll.

Fox had to think fast or die. He gathered what strength he had left. Then, he hit the shark in the eye. He remembered hearing that this sometimes works. It did. The great white released him.

By then, Fox was bleeding badly, but he got to the water's surface. Fox thought he was finally safe. He was wrong. The great white had come after him.

The shark struck Fox a second time. It pulled him beneath the water. The shark had Fox's diver's belt in his mouth. Fox could not get the belt off. He felt trapped. The diver wondered whether he would drown or be eaten first.

Finally, the belt broke. Fox was able to get to the water's surface again. This time, some people in a boat spotted him. They got him out of the water.

Fox was badly hurt. His chest and stomach were ripped open. One of his lungs was injured, as well. Doctors operated on him for hours. He needed nearly 500 stitches.

Rodney Fox could have been killed. But he

Great white sharks, like the one that attacked Rodney Fox, have enormous teeth and wide mouths.

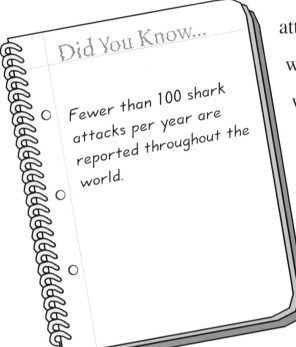

did not blame the shark. The attack did not keep him out of the water, either. Before long Fox went back to diving. He also spent years studying sharks.

At times, people in small fishing boats have barely escaped shark attacks. This happened to a group of travelers in Australia. Without warning, a great white shark appeared behind their boat. It hit the boat a few times. Twice, the shark even shot partly out of the water. The passengers were terrified. The boat's captain thought the great white might have been hungry. He tried to joke about it. He said, "It was just as well nobody fell overboard."

5. A Shark's World

Many people think of sharks as monsters. This is especially true of the great white, tiger shark, and bull shark. But they are not. The sea is their world. They are only trying to survive in it. Scientists have studied these sharks. Here is some of what they know.

Habitat (Where They Live)

Great White Sharks

Great white sharks live in oceans around the world. They swim in temperate (neither hot nor cold) waters. They are often spotted off California's coast.

Sharks do not attack humans out of viciousness. They are only trying to survive in their home, the ocean.

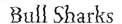

Bull Sharks

Bull sharks are found in warm waters. They usually swim near the shore. The bull shark is unusual. It can also live in fresh water for a time. Fresh waters are rivers and lakes. Some lead into oceans. Bull sharks have been seen in the Mississippi River. Scientists think that bull sharks may be territorial. They may think of a certain area as their own. Anything entering that space may be seen as a threat. This includes human swimmers and divers.

Bull sharks have sometimes been found in the Mississippi River (shown in bright blue).

Tiger Sharks

Tiger sharks swim in tropical (very warm) waters. They are usually found in warm areas around the globe. Sometimes, however, they are also spotted in places that are a bit cooler.

Tiger sharks live near the equator.

Diet (What They Eat)

In some ways, sharks are like most predators. They usually only kill when hungry. How hungry do they get? That depends on the size of their last meal. If their prey was large, some sharks may not get hungry again for a week or two. Sharks have been known to live for months without eating. They survive on the oil in their livers. Humans have never been a regular part of any shark's diet. Here is what is:

Sea otters can be prey for sharks.

Great White Sharks

The great white shark eats otters, sea turtles, seals, sea lions, small whales, and other sea creatures. Great whites are also scavengers. They feed on animals that are already dead. Sometimes, they find dead animals floating in the sea.

Bull Sharks

Bull sharks are fearless hunters. Sometimes they attack

prey as large as themselves. Bull sharks eat fish, sea turtles, sea birds, shellfish, and other sharks.

Tiger Sharks

Tiger sharks are not picky eaters. Their diet mainly includes fish, sea turtles, reptiles, marine mammals, sea birds, and other sharks. These sharks have been called the garbage cans of the sea. License plates, barrels, bottles, and cans have been found in their stomachs.

Sea turtles and shellfish, such as crabs, are a regular part of bull sharks' diets.

Reproduction (How Young Sharks Are Born)

Male and female sharks mate to reproduce. During this process, the male fertilizes eggs inside the female. The fertilized eggs develop into young sharks.

In most sharks, the eggs hatch inside the female's body. The young sharks are born alive. They are called pups. Shark pups look like small adult sharks. Female sharks do not care for their young. The pups swim off as soon as they are born. Sometimes, shark mothers even eat their babies.

Did You Know...

Most sharks are cold-blooded. Their body temperature changes with their surroundings.

Great White Sharks

Great white females birth from two to fourteen young at

a time. Some great white pups may be as large as five feet.

Tiger Sharks

Tiger sharks are born in large groups or litters. There may be from ten to eighty pups.

Bull Sharks

Bull sharks are born in litters of one to thirteen pups. Newborns are about twenty-eight inches long. Bull shark pups are often born in calm bay areas. These tend to be safe places. There are usually few predators around.

Avoiding Shark Attacks

Shark attacks should not scare beach-goers. People do not have to stay out of the water. But the ocean is not a big swimming pool. It is important to be careful. Everyone should follow these safety tips:

❖ Always swim with a group of people. Sharks are more likely to attack a lone swimmer.

❖ Do not swim too far from shore. This makes it harder to get help.

❖ Do not go in the water at dawn or dusk (sunset). Sharks are more active then.

❖ Do not go in the water with a cut. Sharks can smell blood from a great distance.

❖ Do not wear shiny jewelry in the water. Sharks may mistake it for fish scales.

❖ Do not wear brightly colored swimsuits. There have been a number of shark attacks on people wearing bright yellow swimsuits. The color is now known as Yum Yum Yellow.

❖ Do not splash around in the water or swim with pets. Such movements attract sharks.

❖ Do not swim where sea birds are diving. This is a sign that fish are feeding. Sharks are likely to be around, too.

❖ Do not swim between sandbars. Sandbars are

ridges of sand along the ocean's shore. They are built up by waves. Sharks often wait there for prey.

❖ Do not go in the water if sharks are known to be nearby. Leave the water at once if a shark is sighted.

Shark experts say that sharks are in more danger than humans. Their numbers have steadily decreased due to over-fishing. More than 50 million sharks are killed every year. As one shark expert put it, "The real story is not shark bites man. It's man bites shark."

Sharks are in more danger from humans than we are from them.

Fast Facts About
SHARKS

❖ Years ago, sailors did not want sharks following their ships. They thought it was bad luck. So, they sometimes threw one of their own men overboard to please the sharks.

❖ The odds of being killed by a shark are low. You are 30 times more likely to be killed by lightning.

❖ Shark oil is used in many products. These include medicine, soap, makeup, and margarine.

❖ Shark bites have been found on nuclear submarines. These submarines give off a weak electrical charge. The sharks may have mistaken the submarines for their prey.

❖ Dogs are known as man's best friend. Yet, they bite many more people than sharks do.

Glossary

aggressive   Fierce or quick to attack.

ampullae of Lorenzini   A system of tubes through which sharks sense electricity.

cartilage   A strong rubbery bone-like material.

dusk   The time following sunset when it is nearly dark.

equator   An imaginary circular band that divides our planet into two halves, or hemispheres.

fin   A fish body part used to move and steer in the water.

gills   Breathing organs in fish.

lateral line organs   Rows of holes along the sides of a shark's body that sense movement.

limb   A part of the body used to reach or grasp.

litter	A group of animals born at the same time to the same mother.
predator	An animal that hunts other animals for food.
prey	An animal that is hunted as food.
pup	A young shark.
sandbar	Ridges of sand along the ocean's shore built up by waves.
scavenger	An animal that feeds on other animals that are already dead.
shallow	Not very deep.
skeleton	A body's framework of bones or cartilage.
species	Kind or type of plant or animal.
temperate	Not too hot or too cold.
tropical	A hot, wet, rainy area.

Further Reading

Arnold, Caroline. *Giant Shark: Megalodon Prehistoric Super Predator*. New York: Clarion, 2000.

Cerullo, Mary M. *Sharks: Challengers of the Deep*. New York: Cobblehill Books, 1993.

Dubowski, Kathy East. *Shark Attack*. New York: DK Publishing Inc., 1998.

Gibbons, Gail. *Sharks*. New York: Holiday House, 1992.

Pringle, Laurence. *Sharks: Strange and Wonderful*. Honesdale, Penn.: Boyds Mills Press, 2001.

Simon, Seymour. *Sharks*. New York: HarperCollins, 1996.

Woog, Adam. *The Shark*. San Diego, CA: Lucent Books, 1998.

Internet Addresses

Aquatic Network

A Web site filled with information about sea life.

<http://www.aquanet.com>

National Geographic Online

This Web site provides fascinating facts about all sorts of fish and animals. Do not miss the "creature feature" in the special section for kids.

< http://www.nationalgeographic.com>

Sea World/Busch Gardens Animal Information Database

This Web site will take you on an aquatic safari. There is a lot of information about sharks and other sea creatures. A special fun feature is listening to the animal sounds library.

<http://www.seaworld.org>

Index